I0818439

"To Noel-my constant supporter"—**A.G.**


Book design by Marie-Laure Couët

First Edition. Published by Tielmour Press Inc.



The artwork was created digitally.

ISBN: 978-1-998426-30-0 (hbk.)
ISBN: 978-1-998426-33-1 (pbk.)
ISBN: 978-1-998426-31-7 (ebk.)

Tielmour Press books are available at special quantity discount to retailers, professional associations, schools and literacy programs, and other organizations. For details and discount information, contact us at: sales@tielmourpress.com

No generative AI was used in the production of this book.

Library and Archives Canada Cataloguing in Publication

Title: Tricksters, takers, and team players : teaming up for the hunt / [words by] Alisha Gabriel ; [art by] Vivien Sárkány.
Names: Gabriel, Alisha, author. | Sárkány, Vivien, illustrator.
Identifiers: Canadiana (print) 20260180238 | Canadiana (ebook) 20260180246 | ISBN 9781998426300 (hardcover) | ISBN 9781998426331 (softcover) | ISBN 9781998426317 (EPUB)
Subjects: LCSH: Symbiosis—Juvenile literature. | LCSH: Animal behavior—Juvenile literature. | LCSH: Animals—Food—Juvenile literature. | LCSH: Predation (Biology)—Juvenile literature. | LCGFT: Picture books.
Classification: LCC QH548 .G33 2026 | DDC j577.8/5—dc23

## Teaming Up for the Hunt

Alisha Gabriel

Vivien Sárkány

# Animals team up to hunt for many reasons...

for safety,
to capture prey from
hard-to-reach places,
or to find food more easily.

Many animals hunt
for food alone.

Some work with other members of their pack.

But a few hunt with animals from another species.

Some of these partnerships benefit both animals.

Others do not.

# Some animals hunt with a partner.

A coyote and a badger team up to hunt ground squirrels.

When slippery squirrels skitter into their burrows for safety, the badger digs through the dirt with powerful claws.

The coyote guards another exit.

That way, if a ground squirrel tries to escape, the coyote is ready to **pounce!**

If they're lucky, they will both have squirrel for dinner.

# They team up with a nod,

When a grouper is ready to hunt, it nods its head toward a moray eel, and they begin their search.

The grouper does a headstand when it finds prey hiding in a small crevice, and the skinny eel slithers through to flush it out.

Usually, both teammates capture food this way.

a call,

When a hornbill is ready to start foraging for insects and small rodents, it hovers outside a termite mound, making a low chuckling sound.

It keeps calling until its partners, a family of dwarf mongooses, come out.

Finally, the hunt can begin!

They all search for food while keeping watch for birds of prey.

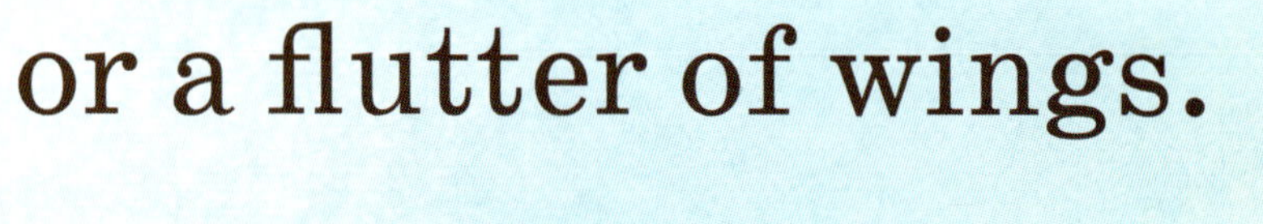

# or a flutter of wings.

In Mozambique, when a man from the Yao community makes a trilling **brrrr-hm** call, a honeyguide flies over and leads him to a beehive.

After the man breaks it open and removes some honey, the bird swoops in to devour bee larvae and wax.

# Some animals follow others to find an easy meal.

When Bewick's swans take a dive, ducks follow.

The swans trample the bottom of the pond with their big, webbed feet, then yank up underwater roots called tubers.

The ducks don't want the tubers, though.

They devour the small animals and plant bits that the swans pull loose from the mud.

# They tag along,

Cattle egrets follow cows as they graze on grasses.

The cows clomp and stomp through the grasses, stirring up insects with every step.

The sharp-eyed cattle egrets snatch the insects out of the air.

wait and watch,

In a forest in India, chital deer follow langur monkeys as they forage for fruit high in the trees.

The deer are in luck!

A few pieces of ripe fruit fall to the ground.

and eat almost anything that lands in the water!

Characid fish in western Brazil swim near the shore while capuchin monkeys scour the trees alongside the river for food.

Fruit, seeds, leaves, and even insects drop into the river as the monkeys gather food.

It's a feast for the fish, too!

# Some animals take food from others.

Orcas follow deepwater fishermen who are searching for tuna.

The orcas listen for the squealing sound of the boat's winch, which signals a catch.

As the workers reel the tuna toward the boat, the orcas dart forward and help themselves to a snack.

# They hide,

A toad watches a horde of army ants search for insects.

They sense a vibration and quickly mob their prey.

Another insect tries to escape from the ants.

Before the ants can attack, the sneaky toad swallows the insect and bounces away.

and trick,

Meerkats search for insect prey.

A drongo screeches a warning, and the meerkats hide.

When the danger passes, a meerkat uncovers a juicy scorpion.

The drongo sounds another warning. This time, it's a lie.

The drongo snatches up the scorpion. What a trickster!

# and steal.

Tunas and dolphins hunt a school of sardines. Together, they force them toward the surface in a bait ball.

The dolphins dart in and out, grabbing sardines.

Near the surface,
seabirds dive
into the water and
gobble them up, too.

Before long, sharks arrive. It’s a feeding frenzy, and sardines are on the menu!

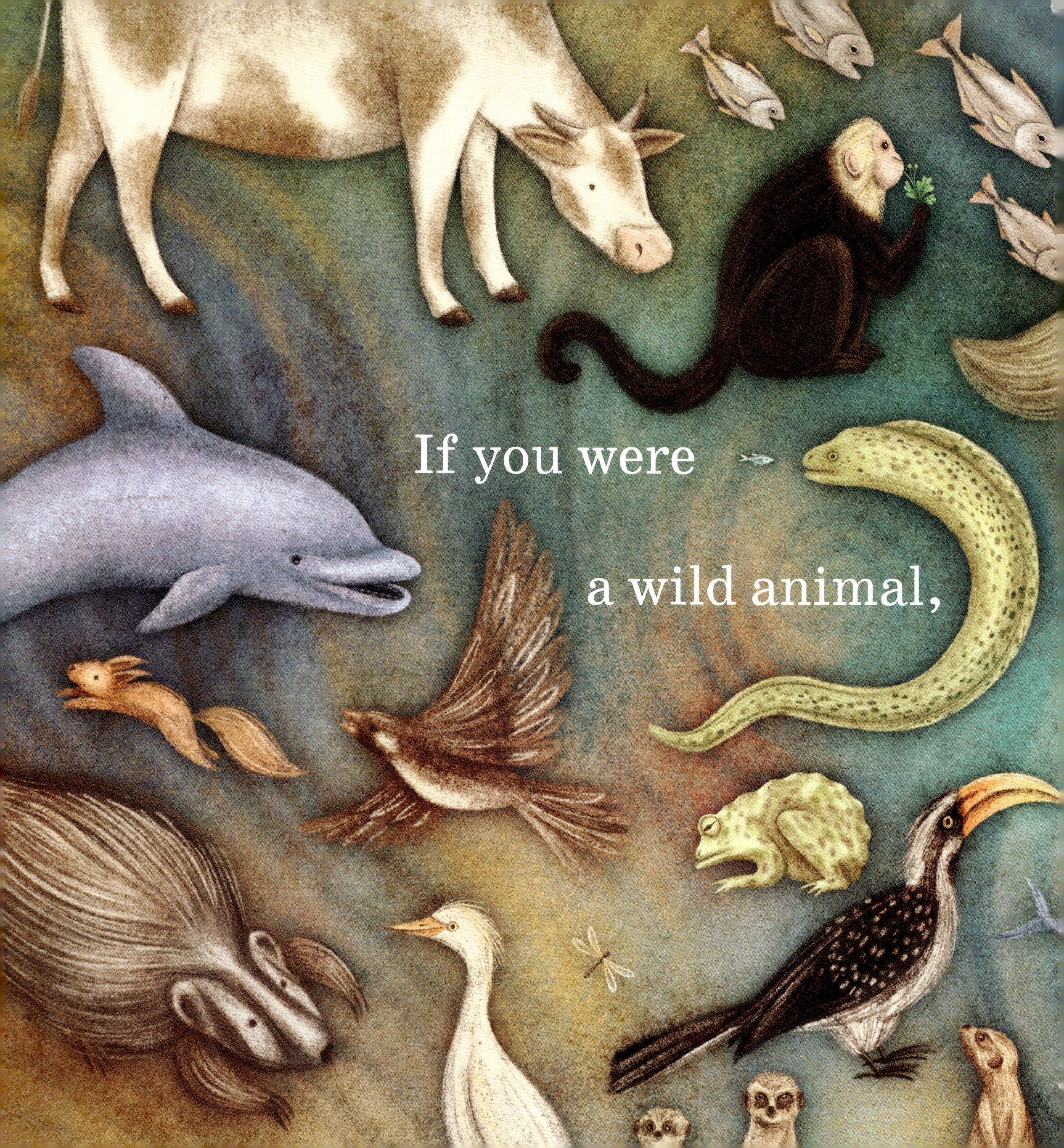

If you were

a wild animal,

who would you choose
as a partner?

## Mixed species groups & Symbiosis

Groups of animals from different species that interact with one another in recurring or extended relationships are part of **mixed species groups**.

Often, the animals in these groups form **symbiotic** relationships, which is when two or more animals work in a way that benefits at least one of them.

## Parasitism

**Parasitism** is a relationship between two or more animals in which some animals benefit while others are harmed. When the drongo makes false-alarm calls in order to steal food from meerkats, it harms the meerkats.

## Mutualism

When both animals benefit, it is called **mutualism**.

Remember the badgers and coyotes? They have a mutualistic relationship because both animals have a better chance of capturing prey when they hunt together.

The grouper and eel fit into this category, as well as honeyguides and humans.

## Commensalism

As predators, cattle egrets and cows fall into a category called **commensalism**.

Although the cows benefit from the birds' pest control, the cattle egrets do not help them find food. On the other hand, they don't cause the cows to lose out on food, either.

## Questions!

Think back to the chital deer and characid fish that follow the monkeys.

Would their relationships be considered mutualism, commensalism, or parasitism? What about the toad and army ants, or the dolphins, sharks, and seabirds?

## Answers:

When we consider their access to food, chital deer and characid fish both have a commensal relationship because they both gain access to more food when they follow monkeys.

Sharks and seabirds have a mostly commensal relationship with the dolphins and tuna as long as there are enough sardines for everyone.

The toad and the ants are in a parasitic relationship because the toad steals food that the ants flushed out.

# Selected Bibliography


Abbott, Alison. "Animal Behaviour: Inside the Cunning, Caring, Greedy Minds of Fish." Nature 521 (2015): 412–414.

Au, D.W.K., and R.L. Pitman. "Seabird Interactions with Dolphins and Tuna in the Eastern Tropical Pacific." Condor 88 (1986): 343–354.

"Clever Fish: Cooperation on the Reef." Nature Video. Footage by Redouan Bshary, Hans Fricke, Alex Vail. May 26, 2015. https://www.nature.com/articles/d41586-019-00363-y.

Goodale, Eben, Guy Beauchamp, and Graeme D. Ruxton. Mixed-Species Groups of Animals: Behavior, Community Structure, and Conservation. London: Academic Press, 2017.

Newton, P.N. "Associations Between Langur Monkeys (Presbytis entellus) and Chital Deer (Axis axis): Chance Encounters or Mutualism?" Ethology 83 (1989): 89–120.

Sabino, Jose, and Ivan Sazima. "Association Between Fruit-Eating Fish and Foraging Monkeys in Western Brazil." Ichthyol. Explor. Freshwaters 10, no. 4 (December 1999): 309–312.

Saha, Purbita, and Claire Spottiswoode. "Meet the Greater Honeyguide, the Bird That Understands Humans." Audubon, August 22, 2016. https://www.audubon.org/news/meet-greater-honeyguide-bird-understands-humans.

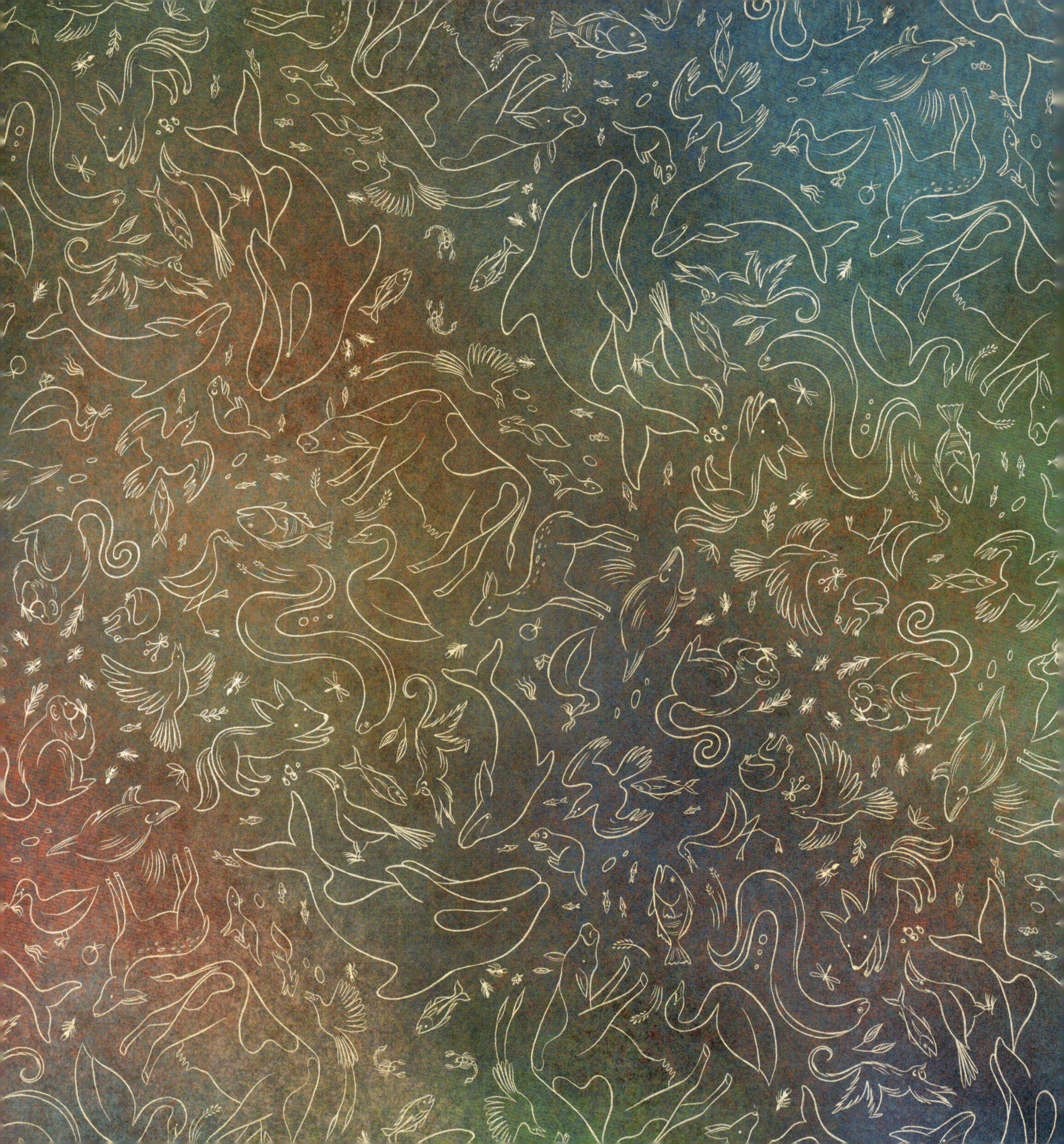